AMAZING ANIMALS
BABOONS
BY MARI BOLTE

CREATIVE EDUCATION • CREATIVE PAPERBACKS

Published by Creative Education and Creative Paperbacks
P.O. Box 227, Mankato, Minnesota 56002
Creative Education and Creative Paperbacks
are imprints of The Creative Company
www.thecreativecompany.us

Design by The Design Lab
Art direction by Graham Morgan
Edited by Jill Kalz

Images by Alamy Stock Photo/Rob Crandall, 19; flickr/Biodiversity Heritage Library, 22–23; Getty Images/Attie Gerber, 8; Pexels/Dario Fernandez Ruz, 18, Frans van Heerden, 10, 13, Jesús Esteban San José, cover, 1, Og Mpango, 6, Ralph, 5, Tayla Walsh, 2; Unsplash/Andrew Liu, 16, Charl Durand, 21, Dawn W, 9, Ramon Vloon, 17; Wikimedia Commons/Bernard DUPONT, 14

Copyright © 2025 Creative Education, Creative Paperbacks
International copyright reserved in all countries.
No part of this book may be reproduced in any form without written permission from the publisher.

Library of Congress Cataloging-in-Publication Data
Names: Bolte, Mari, author.
Title: Baboons / by Mari Bolte.
Description: Mankato, Minnesota : Creative Education and Creative Paperbacks, [2025] | Series: Amazing animals | Includes bibliographical references and index. | Audience: Ages 6–9 | Audience: Grades 2–3 | Summary: "Discover the baboon, one of the world's largest monkeys! Explore the primate's anatomy, diet, habitat, and life cycle. Captions, on-page definitions, an ancient Egyptian animal myth, additional resources, and an index support elementary-aged kids"—Provided by publisher.
Identifiers: LCCN 2024010324 (print) | LCCN 2024010325 (ebook) | ISBN 9798889892403 (library binding) | ISBN 9781682776063 (paperback) | ISBN 9798889893516 (ebook)
Subjects: LCSH: Baboons—Juvenile literature.
Classification: LCC QL737.P93 B65 2025 (print) | LCC QL737.P93 (ebook) | DDC 599.8/65—dc23/eng/20240405
LC record available at https://lccn.loc.gov/2024010324
LC ebook record available at https://lccn.loc.gov/2024010325

Printed in China

Table of Contents

Monkey Around	4
Living Wild	10
Grazing on Grass	12
Family Matters	14
In the Wild	18
A Baboon Tale	22
Read More	24
Websites	24
Index	24

Male hamadryas baboons are known for their pink face and thick, silvery-gray fur.

Baboons are some of the largest monkeys on the planet. Monkeys belong to a group of animals called **primates**. Most primates, including baboons, have long arms and **opposable thumbs**. There are five kinds of baboon. They live in Africa and Arabia.

opposable thumbs thumbs that can move against the fingers of the same hand

primates animals that have hair or fur, large brains, and gripping hands

A baboon's tail can be more than 2 feet (0.6 meter) long.

Most baboons live in open spaces, such as **savannas** or grasslands. Others live in forests or mountains. Baboons spend a lot of time on the ground. But to see danger coming, they need trees or other high places.

savannas grassy plains with few trees

Strong arms and legs help baboons climb trees. So do gripping hands and feet. In trees, baboons find food, sleeping spots, and safety. Baboons have tails, but they can't use them to climb or grab things.

Baboons climb trees to escape leopards, hyenas, and other meat eaters.

A baboon's canines can grow longer than a lion's!

Baboons
have fur in shades of gray, brown, yellow, and red. Their long snout holds lots of teeth. Flat back teeth grind up tough leaves. Sharp **canines** rip and tear. Males use these teeth for fighting.

canines pointed teeth near the front of the mouth

Baboons eat a lot of grass. They also eat tree bark, roots, seeds, and other plant parts. Sometimes small animals, fish, and birds are food, too. Baboons will eat almost anything!

Like humans, baboons use their hands to grab, hold, pick, and peel their food.

13

BABOONS

Baboons live in groups

called troops. Troops may have 10 to 300 members. Males lead and often fight to be in charge. Females stay with their troop their entire lives. Young males must leave to join a different troop.

Females and their offspring form the main part of a baboon troop.

Baby baboons are called infants. At birth, they weigh about 2 pounds (0.9 kilogram). Infants hold tightly to their mother's fur. They drink milk from her all day.

Most baboons have only one infant at a time.

Humans are the biggest danger to baboons. Baboons and people often live near each other. They must share the same water and land. A baboon troop can quickly destroy a farmer's field. Sometimes people poison or kill baboons.

Young male baboons without a troop are more likely to cross paths with people.

Baboons and other kinds of monkey can make humanlike sounds. At least five vowel-like sounds have been recorded. Scientists study baboons—and their sounds—to learn more about these amazing animals.

Baboons pick ticks and other bugs from each other's fur, called grooming.

A Baboon Tale

In ancient

Egypt, the moon god Thoth had the head of a baboon. He was also the god of writing, arithmetic, and knowledge. He gave the Egyptian calendar to the people as a gift. Their calendar is the oldest known calendar in the world. Like the one we use today, it had 365 days grouped into 12 months. The first month of the year was named for Thoth.

Read More

Gillespie, Katie. *Baboon*. New York: Lightbox Learning, 2023.

Hudak, Heather C. *Gorilla, Baboon, and Other Troops*. St. Catharines, Ontario; New York: Crabtree Publishing, 2023.

Websites

Animals A to Z for Kids: Baboon
https://www.animalsatozforkids.com/baboon
Discover fun facts about baboons.

Britannica Kids: Baboon
https://kids.britannica.com/kids/article/baboon/352811
Learn more about baboons.

Note: Every effort has been made to ensure that the websites listed above are suitable for children, that they have educational value, and that they contain no inappropriate material. However, because of the nature of the Internet, it is impossible to guarantee that these sites will remain active indefinitely or that their contents will not be altered.

Index

climbing, 8
dangers, 7, 8, 19
food, 8, 12, 16
fur, 4, 11, 16, 20
groups, 15, 19
homes, 4, 7
humans, 12, 19, 20, 22
infants, 16
sizes, 4, 16
sounds, 20
tails, 7, 8
teeth, 11